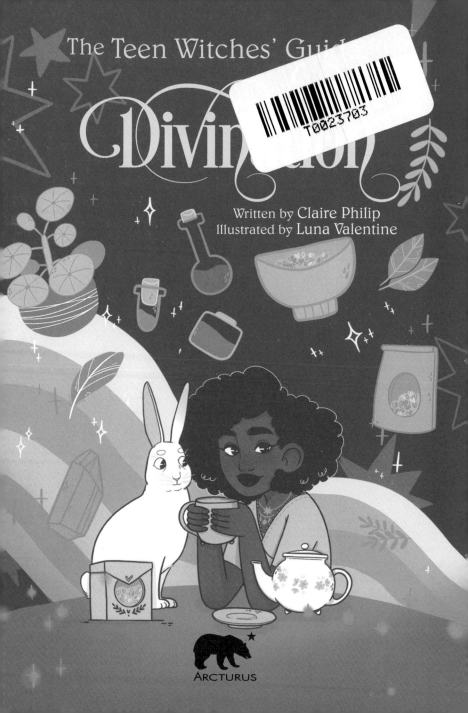

The Teen Witches' Guide

Divination

Written by Claire Philip
Illustrated by Luna Valentine

ARCTURUS

SAFETY WARNING

The ideas, suggestions, and activities in this book are not intended to be a substitute for conventional medical advice. Always consult your doctor or other qualified healthcare professional before undertaking any alternative therapy to ensure that there are no contraindications for your health.

ARCTURUS

This edition published in 2023 by Arcturus Publishing Limited
26/27 Bickels Yard, 151–153 Bermondsey Street,
London SE1 3HA

Text adapted from *The Book of Divination* by Michael Johnstone.

Author: Claire Philip
Illustrator: Luna Valentine
Designer: Rosie Bellwood
Editors: Donna Gregory and Rebecca Razo
Editorial Manager: Joe Harris
Indexer: Lisa Footitt

ISBN: 978-1-3988-2566-6
CH010878NT
Supplier 29, Date 0123, PI 00002502

Printed in China

Contents

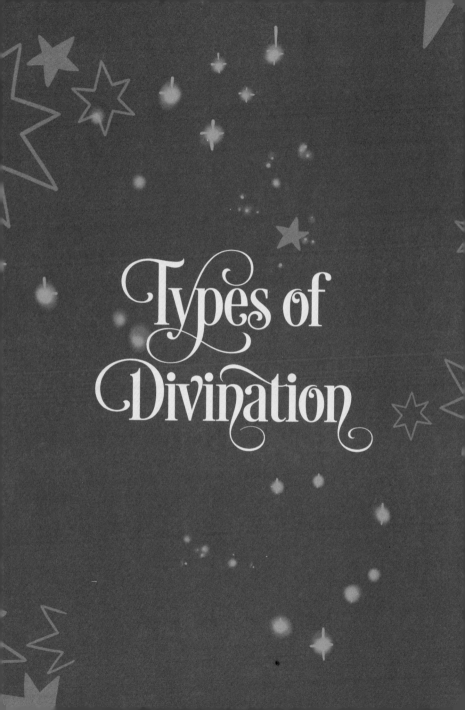

Types of Divination

Introduction

> **Divination is the study of foretelling future events or the discovery of hidden knowledge using magical methods.**

Did you know that most people try to tell the future every single day? It's true! We wonder *if, what, when, how,* and *why* about all kinds of life questions.

There are a variety of divination methods, but here are some of the best known:

> **This book is a resource to help you discover traditional methods of divination so you can begin to sense what could happen in your life.**

AEROMANCY

To perform aeromancy, a person looks to the air and sky for inspiration—especially cloud shapes and comets.

ALEUROMANCY

Have you ever read the message from a fortune cookie? If so, you've tried aleuromancy! This involves baking answers to questions inside pieces of dough. The baked piece is then picked at random by someone with a question!

APANTOMANCY
Some people believe that chance meetings with certain animals, such as black cats, have a deeper meaning.

ASTROLOGY
Astrology, one of the oldest and most popular forms of divination, involves looking to the Moon, Sun, planets, and stars for guidance.

BIBLIOMANCY
To try bibliomancy, ask yourself a question and then open a book at random to any page. The first words you read are your answer!

CARTOMANCY
Ordinary playing cards or specially designed packs, such as the Tarot, can be used to ask questions about the future.

CLAIRAUDIENCE
This word means "clear hearing" and is usually regarded as an extrasensory perception. People who are clairaudient gain insights into the future by listening and hearing.

CLAIRVOYANCE

Those with this extrasensory perception can see pictures of the future either during deep meditation (sometimes called a trance) or in flashes that come out of the blue.

CRYSTALLOMANCY

Crystals are said to have special powers and purposes. Those who use this form of divination focus on a crystal to receive its messages.

DOWSING

This form of divination is sometimes used to find water or precious metals. A forked rod is held over the ground. If the rod vibrates, water or metal may be found!

LECANOMANCY

In this form of divination, people gaze into a basin of water in much the same way that crystallomancers focus on crystals. As they focus, they hope to receive solutions to the questions that they are pondering.

NUMEROLOGY

One of the best-known methods of divination, numerology is the interpretation of numbers, dates, and the numerical value of letters.

ONEIROMANCY

This is the official term for the interpretation of dreams. It is one of the oldest forms of divination.

PALMISTRY

Experts in this ancient art use the lines, mounds, and shape of the hands, fingers, and nails to assess someone's character and predict their future.

PSYCHOGRAPHY

Also called automatic writing, this involves a person writing while they are in a trance-like state.

SCIOMANCY

Involves communicating with spirit guides who inhabit the unseen world.

TASSEOGRAPHY

This is the official term for reading tea leaves.

The Tarot

Introducing The Tarot

The Tarot is a deck of 78 illustrated cards that are used to decipher what is going on in a person's life, as well as helping them work out what may happen next!

The images on the Tarot cards are universal symbols that represent a journey we all walk. This journey is our own heroic path through life. Some of the images can be worrying at first; however, as we learn the deck, we discover that each card represents a necessary stage in the creation process—as well as the process of becoming a fully mature adult.

When learning
the Tarot, it is a good idea
to study the meanings of the
cards and then develop your
own interpretation. Over time,
this will help you develop
your intuition.

Today, there are hundreds of different Tarot designs
to choose from, many of which have a theme or
specific purpose. They are often based on one of the
most popular sets of Tarot cards called the Rider-
Waite-Smith pack, also known as the
Rider-Waite pack.

TAKING CARE OF YOUR DECK
Part of the ritual of using a deck is to treat it with
great care. Keep it somewhere private whenever it is
not in use. Ideally, only you should touch your deck,
although you can ask someone else to shuffle it if you
are doing a reading for them.

THE MAJOR AND MINOR ARCANA

The Tarot is divided into the Major Arcana and the Minor Arcana. Arcana means "mysterious" or "secret." The Major Arcana includes 22 picture cards numbered 0–21. They start with the Fool card at 0 and follow his journey to the World card at 21.

Each card marks an important stage in the Fool's journey. The whole deck marks one complete creative cycle.

THE MAJOR ARCANA CARDS:

0 – The Fool
1 – The Magician
2 – The High Priestess
3 – The Empress
4 – The Emperor
5 – The Hierophant
6 – The Lovers
7 – The Chariot
8 – Strength
9 – The Hermit
10 – Wheel of Fortune
11 – Justice
12 – The Hanged Man
13 – Death
14 – Temperance
15 – The Devil
16 – The Tower
17 – The Star
18 – The Moon
19 – The Sun
20 – Judgment
21 – The World

THE MINOR ARCANA

The Minor Arcana is divided into four suits—wands, cups, swords, and pentacles. Like ordinary playing cards, they start with an ace and then run from 2–10. There are also four court cards: a page, a knight, a queen, and a king.

Wands

represent action, willpower, creativity, energy, and passion. They correspond to the element of fire and the season of spring.

Cups

represent emotions, love, relationships, sensitivity, and fulfillment. They correspond to the element of water and the season of summer.

Swords

represent ideas, intellect, communication, conflict, resolution, and change. They correspond to the element of air and the season of autumn.

Pentacles

represent security, money, achievement, stability, and the living world. They correspond to the elements of earth and the season of winter.

THE COURT CARDS

Kings
represent authority, power, leadership, achievement, and responsibility.

Queens
represent care-giving figures of authority who offer wisdom, confidence, and protection.

Knights
represent action and people who act rashly.

Pages
represent the potential of youth and dreams. They can also be messengers.

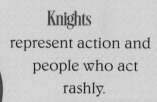

Your First Tarot Spread

The three-card spread is one of the simplest starter spreads and will get you familiar with reading the cards. Before you start, loosely shuffle the deck while focusing on the question you want answered. Then, either cut the deck three times, or fan it out on a tabletop and choose three cards at random.

1 PAST

2 PRESENT

3 FUTURE

The first card you pull represents the past; the second card represents the present; and the third card represents the future. For each card, study the image on the front. What can you see? Look up the meaning of the card, and then reflect on how it could relate to your life.

For an easier reading, start
with a single card.
Quiet your mind, and ask
the deck to show you the
card that can best guide you
in relation to your question;
then select a card.

Reading Tea Leaves

Introducing Tea Leaves

According to legend, the first cup of tea happened by chance—leaves blew into an outdoor cooking pot of water in China and made a brew! It is thought that the tradition of reading tea leaves developed soon after, as early as 3000 BCE.

After the first cup of tea was made, tea drinking—and using tea leaves for divination—spread throughout the Far East and India. From there, it came to Europe. In Britain, it was an expensive luxury—often kept under lock and key.

The practice of reading the leftover remnants from a drink began earlier than the discovery of tea. The ancient Greeks likely used wine for the same purpose.

People who read tea leaves often have their own methods for doing so—and their own interpretations of what they see. Some people pour the tea into a cup through a strainer and examine what remains in the strainer. Others look at the remnants left inside the cup after the drink has been consumed—this is the method we use here.

WHAT DO YOU NEED?

A kettle, a teapot, water, white cups and saucers, and some loose tea leaves.

The best tea leaves to use for divination are traditional varieties, such as Earl Grey or Darjeeling, because they have separate, firm leaves.

PREPARING THE TEA

1. First, boil a kettle of water; then carefully pour it into a teapot—ask an adult to help you with this!

2. Add one teaspoon of tea leaves per person to the pot, plus one extra.

3. Leave the tea to brew for three minutes. Concentrate on your question during this time.

4. Pour the tea into a plain white cup. When it's cooled down, drink the tea while still holding the question in your mind.

5. When there is a small amount of tea left (about a tablespoon), hold the cup in your left hand and carefully swirl the leftovers around three times.

6. Place the cup upside down on its saucer and let the remaining liquid drain away.

7. Hold the cup upright, and examine the patterns the leaves have made inside the cup. Use the following pages to help you interpret your findings!

THE FOUR PARTS OF THE CUP

To start your reading, imagine that your cup is a compass divided into four equal parts, with north at the top, south at the bottom, west to the left, and east to the right. Start with the handle positioned west. Next, examine where most of the leaves have gathered in the cup.

- The area of the cup closest to the handle (west) represents you, or the person asking the questions. Leaves that gather here represent home, family, and close friends.
- The side opposite the handle (east) represents acquaintances, school or work, travel, and other matters outside the home. Lots of leaves gathered here suggest that these things are important to the seeker.

- The area to the north stands for the past. Lots of leaves here indicate that things unresolved in the past are affecting your life.
- The area to the south represents upcoming events and people who are about to have an influence on you. If there aren't leaves here, you are more concerned with the present or the past than with the future.

As well as being divided into these four areas, the cup can be read from the top (near the rim) to the bottom. Shapes close to the rim indicate the present (the coming days and weeks). Leaves toward the bottom indicate the distant future (the coming months and years).

In the Romany tradition, the rim of the cup means joy, while the bottom means sorrow.

An A–Z of Shapes

Shapes and symbols can mean different things to different readers depending on their beliefs, so always listen to your intuition. This A–Z guide to some common symbols will help you get started. If you disagree with a meaning, think about what seems right to YOU.

ANCHOR

If you are having a bumpy ride through life, things will soon be more stable.

ANGELS

Good news is on its way!

ANTS

These insects represent hard work—perhaps you will be working on a project.

ARCHES

Someone could be about to extend a hand of friendship.

ARROWS

To some, arrows signal bad news, but to others they are a sign of good news, especially around money.

BAGGAGE

Bags can mean a trip is in the future. It can also mean you are holding onto "emotional baggage" that needs to be released.

BALLS

If you see a ball, you will soon be bouncing back from difficulties.

BALLOONS

These suggest that any troubles that float into your life will soon drift off again.

BEARS

A friend will be able to give you strength during a time of need.

BEES

A change is in store.

BIRDS

If the birds are flying away from the handle, a departure could be imminent. If they are flying toward the handle, an opportunity is on the way!

BOATS

An important discovery is on the horizon.

BOOKS

If the book is open, exciting surprises are coming. A closed book can mean a delay of some kind.

BOOTS

Caution could be needed.

BOTTLES

A full bottle is a sign to channel energy into a new project, while an empty one can signify exhaustion.

BRIDGES

An opportunity for success.

BROOMS

A good clear-out or cleaning might be in order!

BUILDINGS
A move might be
forthcoming.

BUTTERFLIES
Simple pleasures
are about to flutter into
your life.

CASTLES
Circumstances are about
to improve, especially if
you are desiring some
luxury.

CATS
Many believe that cats
can symbolize treachery.
Surely not kitty!

CHAINS
Creating links with other
people will strengthen
your sense of purpose.

CHERRIES
A victory of some kind is
yours for the taking.

CLOUDS
Doubts may be clouding
your life, but they will
eventually clear.

CLOVER
Good luck is on its way!

COINS
Money is making its
way to you.

COWS
These animals symbolize
wealth and tranquility.

DAFFODILS
Wealth is waiting around
the corner.

DAGGER

A warning of potential danger.

DICE

It could be time to take a risk—so roll the dice!

DOGS

Good friends are coming your way.

DONKEYS

Be patient, and things will work out.

DOORS

An open door can indicate an exciting step into the future. A closed door suggests that now is not the right time.

DUCKS

You may soon discover your natural role in life.

DRUMS

A call to action.

EGGS

A new opportunity awaits.

ELEPHANTS

These majestic creatures signify wisdom and success.

ENVELOPES

Good news of some kind
is on its way.

EYES

Act carefully over the
coming weeks.

FACES

Smiling faces are a good
sign, but frowning faces
can signal opposition.

FEATHERS

Something may upset
you, but it should not be
taken too seriously.

FEET

You may make an
important decision—
soon and quickly!

FENCES

Limitations may be
imposed on you.

FISH

You might need to
act courageously to
overcome obstacles.

FLIES

These insects represent
small but constant
annoyances.

FLOWERS

Either a single flower or a bloom predicts a celebration. They can also signify that you are about to be showered with small acts of kindness.

FROGS

You have a great knack for fitting in, no matter where you are.

FOUNTAINS

Success is in store!

FOXES

These animals signify foresight and indicate that stealth may be needed to achieve an aim, but not at the expense of honesty.

FRUIT

A symbol of prosperous times!

GATES

When open, prosperity and happiness lie ahead. When closed, they could be a warning of loss.

GIANTS

A person with a dominant personality is about to come into your life.

GRAPES

This fruit symbolizes prosperity and good health.

GRASS

You may have an inner restlessness of some kind.

GUITARS

These instruments can predict romance—or an irritable nature.

HAMMOCKS

A desire to opt out of responsibility and take things easy.

HANDS

Open and outstretched hands can mean a new friendship. Closed hands might mean that someone could be uncharacteristically mean.

HEADS

Be on the lookout for new opportunities.

HEARTS

A new friendship is around the corner, and it could lead to love! Hearts also indicate that family situations are developing and that they will need careful management.

HILLS

A warning that your path may become blocked, but that problems will be overcome.

HORSESHOES

These are a general sign of good luck.

HOUSES

Either some domestic matters are about to take up your time, or there is nothing to fear—houses are also indicative of security.

ICEBERGS

Someone you know has hidden depths.

INITIALS

Initials represent the people that they stand for, and any shapes nearby refer to them.

JEWELS

A very generous gift might be in your future!

JUGS

If full, life is filled with good health. If empty, money might be frittered away.

KEYS

A sign of new opportunities and independence.

KITES
Aspirations are very likely to be successful.

LADDERS
An advancement of some kind is on the horizon.

LEAVES
A welcome sign that good fortune is on its way.

LINES
These have different meanings, depending on whether they are straight, slanting, or curvy. Straight lines suggest progress in life; slanting lines can mean a failure; curved lines can predict a disappointment.

LIONS
You have powerful friends!

LIZARDS
Get in touch with your instincts, and trust what they tell you.

MAPS
After a long period of uncertainty, life is going to get back on an even keel.

MICE

This is not the time to be timid!

MIRRORS

You are acting vain or feel that life is passing you by.

MOUNTAINS

Signals more serious obstacles than those indicated by hills. Mountains also symbolize high ambitions.

NECKLACES

You may have a secret admirer! If the necklace is broken, it could mean a friendship is about to end.

NETS

These can be a sign that you are feeling trapped or worried about a new venture.

NUMBERS

One – creativity, energy, new beginnings.
Two – duality and rivalry.
Three – marriage.
Four – work with the resources that are available.
Five – clear communication is needed.
Six – peaceful, happy times.
Seven – the unconscious world; time to put things into perspective.
Eight – suggests following convention.
Nine – self-interest.

OSTRICHES

Suggests that you might bury your head in the sand.

PADLOCKS

When closed, padlocks suggest that unspoken concerns might be a problem. When open, they offer the chance to get out of a difficult situation.

PARROTS

Needless chatter is clouding the real issues. Say no to gossip.

PEACOCKS

Your desire for a more luxurious lifestyle may be fulfilled!

PIGS

Overindulgence could lead to poor health, or you may have a particularly generous friend.

PIPES

If careful thought is given to a problem, you'll find a solution.

PLANE

A journey that might be linked with disappointment in some way; also, represents a new project or a rise in status.

QUESTION MARKS

This symbol may suggest hesitancy and caution for the coming days.

RABBITS
Speed is of the essence!

RAINBOWS
Some wishes may be fulfilled; others may have to be put on hold.

RAVENS
A warning may be coming to you—make sure you listen to it.

ROADS
A new path is about to appear in your life! If the road has a fork, a choice will have to be made.

ROCKS
The path ahead has obstacles, but they can be overcome without much difficulty.

SHELLS
Good news is coming! Shells indicate intuitive wisdom and the need to follow your instincts.

SHIPS
Cast your worries overboard!

SNAKES
It is time to shed any current burdens and slide toward the future.

SQUARES
Protection is there if you need it.

SQUIRRELS
People who save for the future worry less than people who spend as they go.

THE SUN
Murky skies of disappointment will soon clear.

SWORDS
Prepare yourself for arguments!

TELESCOPES
Answers to current mysteries will soon be revealed.

TENTS
A love of adventure, but also an unsettled life.

TOWERS
You may be feeling restricted in some way.

TREES

A growth of prosperity
is coming.

TRIANGLES

This shape can mean
unexpected success
or unexpected failure,
depending on which way it
is pointing. Upward is good;
downward is not.

UNICORNS

These magical creatures
promise an unusual and
unexpected opportunity.

VOLCANOES

You may soon erupt with
anger, especially if you are
trying to hold it in.

WATERFALLS

These bring prosperity.

WHALES

These marine mammals
promise the successful
fulfillment of a big
undertaking.

WHEELS

If they are complete, good
fortune will roll in. If broken,
disappointments may loom.

WINDOWS

If open, they mean good
luck. If closed, they mean
bad luck.

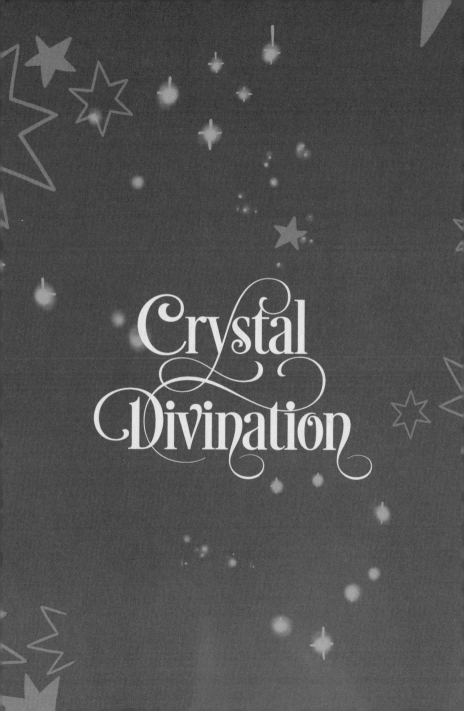

Crystal Divination

Introducing Crystal Gazing

Crystal gazing has a long tradition as part of scrying: using crystals, mirrors, flames, and water to see into the future.

Crystal gazing has its roots in prehistory. If a tribe member had a gift for seeing into the future, they would use their talents to predict what could happen next for the benefit of the group. They didn't always use crystals for this. A stretch of calm, still water also worked well.

Nostradamus, a famous seer, would sit alone at night and gaze into a bowl of water held in a brass tripod and lit by a candle. On the water's surface, he saw visions that are still relevant today.

USING A CRYSTAL BALL

Traditionally, a ball used for crystal gazing should be a gift from someone else with a talent for divination, but these days they can easily be bought from a spiritual shop. Clear or smoky quartz, beryl, obsidian—even glass—are the most popular.

If you decide to buy a crystal ball, you need to find one that feels just right for you. Enter the shop in a calm, peaceful state. Then look at and handle several different balls. As you do, ask yourself:

- How does the crystal ball feel in my hand?
- Does it feel like it "belongs" with me?
- Are there any shapes, blemishes, or bubbles that could be distracting if I were to gaze into it?

Most people find that when they go to buy their crystal ball, they keep returning to one no matter how many they look at. If that happens, you've found your ball!

Doctor John Dee, whose divination talents were praised by Queen Elizabeth I, used a shiny black obsidian mirror to help him make prophecies.

How To Crystal Gaze

To prepare the ball, wash it in a light solution of vinegar and water, and then polish it with a soft cloth. When not in use, it should be kept out of sunlight, which affects its sensitivity. No one other than you should handle your crystal ball.

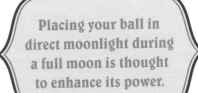

Placing your ball in direct moonlight during a full moon is thought to enhance its power.

1. In a quiet, gently lit room, relax your mind by taking long, slow, deep breaths while holding your crystal ball.
2. Place the ball on a piece of black silk or velvet—ideally, partially surrounded by a small curtain or screen.
3. Stare at the crystal until your eyes go out of focus. Don't force anything to happen—just gaze.
4. If you start to see any images forming in your mind's eye or even on the crystal itself, take notice and make notes in your journal. No effort should be made to keep the images—they should be allowed to come and go.
5. During your first session, stop after ten minutes. Over time you can build this up (to no longer than one hour).

Once you've learned how to hold this relaxed, receptive state, you'll be able to maintain it with another person in the room. If they speak quietly and softly, you'll still be able to keep your intuitive mind active.

When gazing into a crystal ball, your rational, logical mind needs to completely relax, and your intuitive mind needs to be active.

Chinese Astrology

Twelve-Year Cycles

In China, astrology and the *I Ching* (see pages 60–79) are part of everyday life for millions of people.

Chinese astrology is based on a twelve-year cycle. Each year within the cycle is named after an animal, which rules for twelve months before the next animal takes over. Legend has it that Buddha invited all animals to celebrate the New Year, but only twelve arrived! Buddha rewarded those who came by naming a year after them.

THE SIGNS

The Chinese calendar is a combination of lunar (Moon) and solar (Sun) activity, which means the starting and finishing dates of each year vary from year to year. The Chinese New Year starts on the first day of the first new moon, usually at the end of January or the end of February.

The twelve years are the Rat, the Ox, the Tiger, the Rabbit, the Dragon, the Snake, the Horse, the Ram, the Monkey, the Rooster, the Dog, and the Pig. People born in the year of a particular animal are thought to possess that animal's qualities.

YIN AND YANG

The years and months of the Chinese calendar are assigned Yin and Yang aspects. Yin is soft, dark, cold, and wet. Yang is hard, bright, hot, and dry. In traditional Chinese medicine, perfect health for both body and mind depends on achieving a balance between the two.

THE FIVE ELEMENTS

As well as an animal, each year is assigned one of the following five elements: Water, Fire, Earth, Metal, or Wood. This means that while two Rabbit personalities may share common traits, they could be influenced by different elements. For example, a Fire Dragon will be different to an Earth Dragon, and a Metal Monkey will be different to a Water Monkey.

ELEMENT	PERSONALITY TRAITS
Metal	Metal people tend to be rigid and not give in easily. They insist on honesty and expect a lot from their relationships. They also have strong characters and can be dominating.
Water	Water lends creativity to a sign. Water people are compassionate, flexible, and easily influenced.
Wood	Wood personalities are considerate, warm, generous, and cooperative. They try extremely hard to see another person's point of view.

Fire	The most dynamic of the elements! Fire people are principled, but they can be inflexible, too.
Earth	Earth people are hard workers, and they like other people to see their point of view. They are patient—and stubborn.

THE RAT

Charming, clever, quick-witted, and sociable are all words that describe the Rat! They are naturally curious and want to know as much as they can about absolutely everything. Those born under this sign are talkative, practical, and adaptable.

YEARS – 1948, 1960, 1972, 1984, 1996, 2008, 2020

THE OX

People born in the year of the Ox are intelligent and often care deeply about the environment. They love their homes and families. Ox personalities can be possessive, but they make excellent team players and always pull their weight.

YEARS – 1949, 1961, 1973, 1985, 1997, 2009, 2021

THE TIGER

Those born under the sign of the Tiger tend to be charismatic, brave, and competitive. They see themselves as natural leaders, yet they can be loners in some areas of their lives. Tiger types love to have their efforts noticed—conquest is the name of the game, and they rarely fail.

YEARS – 1950, 1962, 1974, 1986, 1998, 2010, 2022

THE RABBIT

Rabbit personalities can be both outgoing and shy! They are afraid of confrontation and will dig themselves into a burrow until an issue has passed. If you know someone who observes from the side-lines at a party but who loves to gossip on the phone straight after, they could be a rabbit!

YEARS – 1951, 1963, 1975, 1987, 1999, 2011, 2023

THE DRAGON

People born under this sign have an intuitive ability to understand any situation, which means that they can influence events around them. Dragons are self-confident and start projects with boundless enthusiasm—but they often abandon them to move on to the next best thing.

YEARS – 1952, 1964, 1976, 1988, 2000, 2012, 2024

THE SNAKE

Snake types are hypnotic, charming, and wise, but they can also be naïve. They are always planning their next move, right down to the last detail. They absorb facts and information easily, but can also cook up original, artistic ideas.

YEARS – 1953, 1965, 1977, 1989, 2001, 2013, 2025

THE HORSE

Those born under the Horse are as sociable and hard-working, as the animal itself. Their downside? They can develop strong prejudices and become intolerant of others.

YEARS – 1954, 1966, 1978, 1990, 2002, 2014, 2026

THE RAM

The Ram (also referred to as the Goat) likes everything to be in its proper place. They are the realists of the Chinese Zodiac and like things to run smoothly. The word "inspiring" is not one that could be applied to most Rams, but when it comes to researching or planning, Rams cannot be beaten.

YEARS – 1955, 1967, 1979, 1991, 2003, 2015, 2027

THE MONKEY

Monkeys in the wild are agile and constantly moving, which eventually tires them out. It's the same with their Zodiac counterparts. Always on the go, inventive, and great fun to be with, they can also feel very low for short periods of time.

YEARS – 1956, 1968, 1980, 1992, 2004, 2016, 2028

THE ROOSTER

A natural leader, the Rooster is alert to new opportunities, and is also often the first person to see a problem looming on the horizon. Others often see the Rooster as over-confident, forever shouting about their own achievements.

YEARS – 1957, 1969, 1981, 1993, 2005, 2017, 2029

THE DOG

Loyal, protective, and fearless are all terms to describe the Dog. They get involved in all kinds of things, often without thinking of the consequences. They want results, and they want them now! They make great friends and are quick to show affection.

YEARS – 1958, 1970, 1982, 1994, 2006, 2018, 2030

THE PIG

The last sign in the twelve-year cycle, Pigs are born at a time when new horizons beckon. They are creative and intelligent and are only too happy to take the world as they find it. Pig types are generous and often enjoy a lively social life.

YEARS – 1959, 1971, 1983, 1995, 2007, 2019, 2031

The I Ching

Introducing The *I Ching*

The *I Ching* (also called *The Book of Changes*) is made up of 64 hexagrams, each with a different meaning. Those who study this form of divination use the *I Ching* to understand current situations and predict the future.

Legend has it that around 5000 BCE, the first Chinese Emperor, Fu Hsi, was meditating by a river, when an animal that looked like a dragon rose from the water. Fu Hsi noticed that there were lines on its scales. After studying them, he felt as though he had gained wisdom, so he began drawing a series of broken and unbroken lines, using the scales as his guide. These became the eight trigrams—the foundation of the *I Ching*.

A trigram is made up of three lines. The unbroken lines are Yin energy, and the broken lines are Yang energy.

Thousands of years after Fu Hsi drew the original eight trigrams, a man named King Wen devised the 64 hexagrams. His son, Tan, interpreted each of their meanings in full.

CASTING A HEXAGRAM

The most common way to cast a hexagram is to use coins that have markings, such as heads or tails, on either side.

- First, hold the question you want answered in your mind.
- Next, cast your three coins six separate times. Each time, note down how many heads or tails landed. Heads are worth three; tails are worth two.
- Add up the value of the coins after each toss. If the value of the number is odd, draw one unbroken line. If the value of the line is even, draw a broken line, with the break in the middle.
- Repeat this process six times, drawing the lines from the bottom to the top.

Combinations	Type of Line
2 tails and 1 head = 5	Odd number = unbroken line
2 heads and 1 tail = 8	Even number = broken line
3 tails = 6	Even number, but as a "changing line," it converts to its opposite: unbroken line (see next page)
3 heads = 9	Odd number, but as a "changing line," it converts to its opposite: broken line (see next page)

I CHING HEXAGRAM TABLE—THE 64 SYMBOLS

- Each line combination matches one of the *I Ching* hexagrams. Review the meanings by pairing the number of the hexagram to the descriptions on pages 66–79.

- Changing lines—Three tails, (resulting in a six) or three heads (resulting in a nine) are referred to as "changing." These should be converted to their opposite hexagram. For example, the number six (an even number) would be a broken line; change it to an unbroken line. The number nine (an odd number) would be an unbroken line; change it to a broken line. Now you can look up their meanings!

- Trigrams run in two directions and are designated upper and lower. Each represents one of the following eight elements: Heaven, Earth, Thunder, Water, Mountain, Wind, Fire, and Lake.

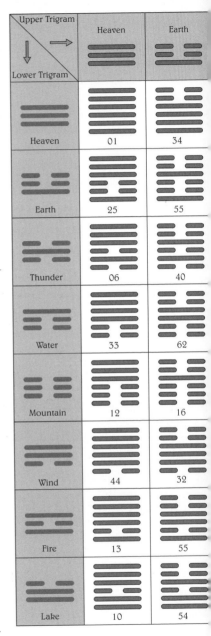

Upper Trigram → / Lower Trigram ↓	Heaven	Earth
Heaven	01	34
Earth	25	55
Thunder	06	40
Water	33	62
Mountain	12	16
Wind	44	32
Fire	13	55
Lake	10	54

Thunder	Water	Mountain	Wind	Fire	Lake
05	26	11	09	14	43
03	27	24	42	21	17
29	04	07	59	64	47
39	52	15	53	56	31
08	23	02	20	35	45
48	18	46	57	50	28
63	22	36	37	30	49
60	41	19	61	38	58

The Meanings

1. CHI'EN—THE CREATIVE

Success is guaranteed due to your strength, power, and persistence. Plans can be continued.

2. K'UN—THE RECEPTIVE

The future can be viewed with confidence! Your success may lie in other people's hands, so listen to advice.

3. CHUN—INITIAL DIFFICULTY

Opportunities that arise should be carefully considered. If help is needed, don't be afraid to ask for it.

4. MENG—INNOCENCE

There may be a lack of experience—or even wisdom. Listen to the advice of more worldly people, but remain enthusiastic and don't give up.

5. HSU—WAITING

Patience is a virtue. Help will be at hand when the time is right, so don't force the pace. Let go of worry.

6. SUNG—CONNECTION

Compromise is the keyword now. If criticism is offered, accept it. Listen to advice, and things will improve.

7. SHIH—THE ARROW

Ask for respect, and your request will be received. Progress will come, but probably after a struggle and after receiving good advice from a wise person.

8. PI—UNION

This is the time to build up strong bonds with others by sharing your experiences.
Help them, and you will be helping yourself.

9. HSIAO CH'U—TAMING FORCE

Now is the time to use your strength and power to clear small blocks from your path.

10. LU'—TREADING CAREFULLY

Stick to the path you have chosen and press forward without hesitating.

11. T'AI—TRANQUILITY

Good fortune and harmony are all around, so enjoy them and share them with others. This is a good time for future planning and steady progress.

12. P'I 1—STAGNATION

This is not the time to force the pace even if you are sure of success. This is a time for humility.

13. T'UNG JEN—COMPANIONSHIP

There are rewards from working with others if everyone sticks to the tasks they have been assigned. This is a time for sharing. Travel is also indicated.

14. TA YU—GREAT POSSESSION

If you work hard and prepare for the future, success is yours for the taking.

15. CH'IEN 2— HUMILITY

Be modest and others will give you the help you need. Harmony is everything—it is vital to remain tolerant of others, no matter how bad their actions may appear.

16. YU— HAPPINESS

Sell yourself, without necessarily believing what you say. This is a good time to plan. Remember, money isn't everything—spiritual health is just as important.

17. SUI—FOLLOWING

Now is the time to take a back seat and let others take charge. Stay flexible and avoid conflict. Relax, but don't let your goals slip from your view.

18. KU—DISRUPTION

Honesty is the best policy. When you move forward, do so with care. If you have made mistakes in the past, now is the time to make things better.

19. LIN—APPROACH

Let caution be your buzzword, moving forward with care and consideration of others. Rash decisions are costly right now.

20. KUAN—OBSERVING

A good time to plan and for looking beneath the surface at things. Joint ventures could pay off.

21. SHIH HO—BITING THROUGH

Be positive about the success that has been achieved. And don't let the negativity of others affect you.

22. P'I 2—ADORNMENT

Keep a rein on spending. Manage everything in small stages. Now is not the time for big changes.

23. PO—STRIPPING AWAY

The odds are not currently on your side. There are disruptions ahead, and change is in the air. Wait and do what is needed to cope.

24. FU—RETURNING

Take caution, particularly around anything new. It is a time for patience and for timing the path ahead. Old energies will be refreshed and new ones will appear.

25. WU WANG—CORRECTNESS

Everything has its limits. Selflessness and simplicity are key now. Remember that problems are usually temporary.

26. TA CH'U— TAMING FORCE

Work is hard and progress is slow, but luck is on your side, and success is on the way—especially if you learn from past mistakes.

27. I 1—NOURISHMENT

Take care, not only about what you eat and drink, but also about what you say. Build up strength, bide your time, and keep ambitions in check.

28. TA KUO—EXCESS

This is a time for extraordinary action. Listen to your inner voice. Success is there waiting for you to grasp it!

29. K'AN—THE DEEP

Take care and be on the lookout for pitfalls. Conflict is in the air, so proceed with caution. Have faith in yourself and all will be well.

30. LI—FIRE

Find success by recognizing your limitations. Now is the time to put your intellect to use. Be calm but firm.

31. HSEIN—SENSITIVITY

Be receptive to others' ideas and avoid becoming envious. Help others at every opportunity, but make sure you are being genuine.

32. HENG—PERSISTENCE

Set your course and stay with it. Stick to traditional methods and avoid taking rash action. If others offer advice, listen.

33. TUN—WITHDRAWAL

There may be trouble ahead, but if you judge the right time to withdraw from the situation and are practical, you will weather the storm.

34. TA CHUANG—THE POWER OF GREATNESS

If you make a promise, stick to your word. This is a time of good fortune. If you act wisely, you will benefit from it.

35. CHIN—ADVANCEMENT

This is a time when honesty is the best policy and a time to think of others.

36. MING I—DARKENING OF THE LIGHT

Try not to get bogged down by making too many plans. Do not get discouraged if things don't go your way—it will get better!

37. CHIA JEN—FAMILY

Family matters are current. It could be necessary to show authority. Do so fairly and with tolerance.

38. K'UEI—OPPOSITION

Try to stay in balance by ironing out anything disruptive in your life. It is a good time for starting small projects. Remember, mighty oaks grow from tiny acorns!

39. CHIEN 1—HALTING

Hard times are ahead. The only way to solve them is to face them.

40. CHIEH 1—REMOVING OBSTACLES

A time for action, but without rushing in. Solve the problem and then put it behind you. Resist the temptation to dwell on the past.

41. SUN 1—DECREASE

Cut back on spending, but share what you have with others even if it means making some sacrifices. If you do this willingly, the gain will be yours in the end.

42. I 2—INCREASE

Luck is on your side—you can make plans with confidence that they will be successful. You may make mistakes, but don't worry. All will turn out to your benefit.

43. KUI—BREAKTHROUGH

Take precautions against possible losses, and they will be kept to a minimum. Be firm without being pushy, Try to cultivate friendships—they will blossom.

44. KOU— MEETING

Be resolute. Stand your ground and don't give in, whatever you do. Now is not the time to sign contracts or make agreements.

45. TS'UI—GATHERING TOGETHER

Sincerity and openness will help you to make your relationship especially harmonious now. There may be a bit of a struggle ahead. If you feel left alone with a project, only ask one person for help.

46. SHENG—ASCENDING

Progress might be on the slow side, but you are moving forward. Professional help could be beneficial.

47. K'UN 2—REPRESSION

Things are hard, but stay calm and you will cope. You may have to dig deep into your reserves with determination.

48. CHING—THE WELL

Things are looking up, but remember that nothing lasts forever. Make sure you are sincere in all your dealings, or you'll face the consequences.

49. KO—CHANGE

Big changes regarding opportunities beckon, followed by a series of smaller ones. Remember that money is not the only thing that matters.

50. TING—THE CAULDRON

Lots of little things occur that get you down, but they aren't serious! Life will soon pick up.

58. TUI—THE JOYOUS

Good news and good fortune come your way. People can see just how in tune you are with your spiritual side.

59. HUAN—DISPERSAL

It is a time for reason. Friends from the past could resurface, and strong bonds may be formed.

60. CHIEH 2—RESTRAINT

You may feel trapped in some way, but if you remain calm you will be able to take advantage of new opportunities.

61. CHUNG FU—INNERMOST SINCERITY

Great results come from well thought-out communication. Plans made for the future are likely to succeed.

62. HSIAO KUA—GREAT SMALLNESS

Success doesn't need to come in one big bag. Lots of small packages can be just as rewarding!

63. CHI CHI— COMPLETION

Don't stop working toward your goal simply because you have achieved some success.

64. WEI CHI— BEFORE COMPLETION

Don't make a move until you are certain the time is right; then proceed with care.

Numerology

Introducing Numerology

Pythagoras—the founder of geometry—believed that numbers were the essence of all things. Each one, he taught, had its own unique vibration and specific personality. He also categorized the human soul into nine different types.

The Sun and Moon are allocated two numbers because when the system was made, there were only seven known planets, and all nine numbers needed to be allocated.

Numbers and Western astrology are connected—each of the twelve astrological signs is assigned a planet and a corresponding number.

However, only the numbers 1–9 are used in numerology. Double-digit numbers are reduced to a number between 1 and 9 by adding them together.

For example, 36 would be: $3 + 6 = 9$. In this case, 9 is the numerology number. For double-digit numbers with a zero, you would simply use the number assigned a value. For example, 10 would be: $1 + 0 = 1$.

Western astrology star sign	Ruling planet	Number
Aries	Mars	9
Taurus	Venus	6
Gemini	Mercury	5
Cancer	Moon	2, 7
Leo	Sun	1, 4
Virgo	Mercury	5
Libra	Venus	6
Scorpio	Mars	9
Sagittarius	Jupiter	8
Capricorn	Saturn	9
Aquarius	Saturn	8
Pisces	Jupiter	3

YOUR BIRTH NUMBER

Your birth number reveals your natural powers and abilities —and is often used as an indication of likely career choices. Use the example below to help you figure out your birth number.

Example:
November 16, 2008
November is the eleventh month, so the reduction formula would look like this:
1 + 1 (month) + 1 + 6 (day) + 2 + 0 + 0 + 8 (year) = 19
Continue to reduce until you get to a single digit between 1 and 9:
1 + 9 = 10;
then 1 + 0 = 1

In this example, the number 1 is the birth number.

Once you know your birth number, you can look up its meaning!

ONE

This number is associated with the Sun and the fire signs Leo, Sagittarius, and Aries. It therefore symbolizes creativity and leadership. Being the first number, it is linked with new beginnings, breaks with the past, assertiveness, and masculinity. Their overall impression is action, fitness, and good health.

TWO

Linked to the Moon, now a symbol of femininity, two indicates strong intuition, the power of deep thought, and sensitivity. Twos tend to underestimate themselves—this can lead to them having difficulty standing their ground.

THREE

A mystical number in many cultures. Threes are usually intelligent and wise. They love life, have outgoing personalities, and prefer to be with others. They often have psychic abilities.

FOUR

Another Sun number, Fours often have a tough, aggressive nature but they keep it hidden. They enjoy hard work and the rewards it brings. They can lack confidence in relationships, but they make loyal, lifelong friends.

FIVE

The number of the planet Mercury—messenger to the gods—Fives are mentally and physically always on the move. They are charming and cheerful extroverts who can become anxious and impatient. Their quick minds make them great inventors and writers.

SIX

Six is the symbol of partnership, love, and marriage. Those with this birth number are likely to enjoy loving relationships. They are friendly and introverted, and they enjoy quiet, artistic people. They also love their homes—and getting dressed up.

SEVEN

There are seven days in the week, seven hues in the rainbow, and seven pillars of wisdom— seven might be the most magical of the numbers! Sevens, though, aren't typically magical by nature. They are realists with a warm and cheerful personality.

EIGHT

With Saturn as its associated planet, eight is the number of secrets and dark places. It is symbolic of the good aspects of old age—wisdom and patience— and the unfortunate ones, such as a loss of vitality. People whose birth number is eight mature faster than their peers, and they have strong opinions.

NINE

Mars—the god of War—rules nine, the number of wisdom, virtue, and ignorance. Nine rekindles the life spark, which can make them confident but also accident prone.

YOUR DESTINY NUMBER

This number shows which energy you are likely to use to achieve your goals. When you calculate your destiny number, each letter of your full birth name is given a number. Use the chart below to work out the numbers of your name; then follow the example on page 89 to find the digit.

1	2	3	4	5	6	7	8	9
A	B	C	D	E	F	G	H	I
J	K	L	M	N	O	P	Q	R
S	T	U	V	W	X	Y	Z	

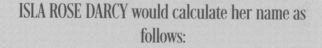

ISLA ROSE DARCY would calculate her name as follows:

$$\text{ISLA} = 9 + 1 + 3 + 1 = 14; \text{ then } 1 + 4 = 5$$
$$\text{ROSE} = 9 + 6 + 1 + 5 = 21; \text{ then } 2 + 1 = 3$$
$$\text{DARCY} = 4 + 1 + 9 + 3 + 7 = 24; \text{ then } 2 + 4 = 6$$

$$5 + 3 + 6 = 14; \text{ then } 1 + 4 = 5.$$

Isla's destiny number is 5.

Name vowel numbers and name consonant numbers provide even deeper readings than destiny numbers. To learn about your external self, add up the vowels in your name; then reduce to a single digit. To learn about your internal self, repeat the process with the consonants in your name.

YOUR NAME VOWEL NUMBER

ONE

suggests an open, confident personality, who might believe they are better than others. This group enjoys money.

TWO

often indicates a lack of self-confidence but also indicates creative talents. They make great therapists and caring medical professionals.

THREE

points to people who enjoy the good things in life and might overindulge! They can be blunt and are natural teachers.

FOUR

indicates responsibility, dependability, and stability but also self-doubt. Fours enjoy structure; they are suited to jobs in the arts, architecture, and design.

FIVE

is often the vowel number for clever, quick-minded people, who enjoy learning languages and acquiring new skills. They may have quick tempers and love to gossip.

SIX

suggests a well-balanced, slightly reserved nature. Sixes are upset by anything unjust and tend to hold back from taking sides.

SEVEN

encourages a bright, creative nature. They can be intellectual but erratic, often abandoning ambitious schemes.

EIGHT

Indicates a conventional nature—someone who is stable and cautious but with a lively imagination. People with this number don't like sudden change.

NINE

Nines see life purely in black and white. They think first and act later, but luckily generosity makes those affected by their rash decisions forgive them quickly.

YOUR NAME CONSONANT NUMBER

ONE

suggests a strong sense of one's own worth. They believe their ideas are the best.

TWO

indicates an active imagination and the tendency to live in a fantasy world.

THREE

points to a passionate nature and a feeling that their beliefs set them apart.

FOUR

says that a creative nature is balanced with common sense, but also warns that persistence might be mistaken for stubbornness.

FIVE

may indicate restlessness and eccentricity. These traits appeal to some and annoy others.

SIX

is a thoughtful number, suggesting a liking of meditation and mysticism—and a dislike of change.

SEVEN

is associated with an instinctive knowledge of how things are or how they should be, and a liking for their own company.

EIGHT

speaks of caution, an unwillingness to take risks, and a dislike of waste—but it also has hints of passion.

NINE

is a number of deep desires often combined with a difficulty expressing them.

Palmistry

Introducing Palmistry

Palmistry is a combination of two ancient divination techniques: chirognomy, which studies a person's character through the shapes and markings of their hand, and chiromancy, which uses that same information to foretell future events.

Palmistry was first used in China more than 3,000 years ago, and it is still popular today.

Psychologist Carl Jung was fascinated by palmistry. He believed that a person's dominant hand represented their outward personality, and the non-dominant hand represented their inner personality.

It's believed that the dominant hand reflects events that have happened in the past and events as they are unfolding in the present. The non-dominant hand, also called your minor hand, offers clues into one's potential and deepest desires.

TYPES OF HANDS

Just as no two people have identical fingerprints, no two people have the same hands! There are, however, six main hand shapes that can tell a lot about a person.

THE PRACTICAL HAND	A nondescript hand with regular features. People with this hand can be impatient and passionate.
THE SQUARE HAND	Square-shaped fingers with a firm palm. People with this hand type are often logical, persistent, and helpful in a crisis.
THE SPATULATE HAND	Wide, irregularly shaped hand with large thumb and flattened fingers. Denotes restlessness and excitability.
THE PHILOSOPHICAL HAND	Long, bony hand with a thick palm and stubby thumb. Denotes wisdom and intelligence.
THE MIXED HAND	A combination of shapes, making it more difficult to interpret. A curved hand can indicate anxiety.
THE GRACEFUL HAND	A long palm and pointed fingers. People with this hand type are intuitive and follow their instincts!

THUMBS

The first thing to look at during a palm reading is the thumb, which represents willpower—nervous people tend to curl it up into their palm.

- Strong, thick thumbs indicate that the person can deal with whatever life throws their way.
- Long thumbs indicate clear, rational thinking and leadership qualities.
- Short thumbs can mean the person is submissive; short, stubby thumbs can indicate aggression.
- A square thumb tip indicates a practical nature, while a rounded tip can mean the person is good with their hands.
- The angle of a thumb gives us information. If it is less than 45 degrees, it can mean the person needs to be in control, whereas an angle of 90 degrees can mean they are charming and outgoing!

READING FINGERS

THE JUPITER FINGER

The first (or index) finger, called the Jupiter finger,
indicates ambition and expansion. A long Jupiter
finger indicates high self-confidence and awareness.
A medium-length Jupiter finger means you are
modest most of the time, but can be confident when
necessary. A short index finger indicates a shy and
self-doubting nature.

THE MIDDLE FINGER

The second (middle) finger, known as Saturn, relates
to judgment and knowledge. Those with long middle
fingers work hard to get ahead, and they usually get
to where they want to go! A medium-length middle
finger, can indicate that you know when it is time
to work and when it is time to play. A short middle
finger can be a sign of carelessness.

THE RING FINGER

The third (ring) finger talks of exploits and
achievements. This finger is often associated with
creativity. If your ring finger is long, you probably
have an artistic nature. A medium-length ring finger
still indicates creativity, but in a more traditional,
conservative sense. A short ring finger means that
there is little creativity.

THE LITTLE FINGER

The little finger, Mercury, has to do with observation and perception. Length here indicates intelligence and excellent communication skills. A medium-length little finger indicates average intelligence, and a short little finger means a tendency toward naïveté.

THE MAJOR LINES

The four most important lines on your hand are the life line, heart line, fate line, and head line. They change over the course of your life.

THE HEART LINE

The heart line is the deep horizontal line at the top of the palm, below the fingers. It runs from the palm's edge to just below the first and middle fingers. It tells you about your emotional energy.

- Long—you are loyal and popular.
- Short—you may have few friends and prefer pets to people!
- Broken line—you express emotion freely, or you hold it in.
- Curves up—you are likely to be romantic.
- Straight—you are nurturing.
- Split line—you have two sides to your personality.

THE HEAD LINE

The head line is the horizontal line that runs parallel to and below the heart line. It shows you how to focus your mental energy.

- Long—you are a deep thinker. You love learning and planning the future.
- Short—you live in the present, find it easy to learn new skills, and don't worry much.
- Straight—you are logical and like facts; you need to experience something in order to believe it.
- Bent line—You are mystical and imaginative.
- Clear, deep line—you are good at concentrating.
- Broken line—indicates difficulty focusing.

THE LIFE LINE

Ideally, the life line is strong and clear. It runs perpendicular to the heart and head lines, curving in a semi-circle from the head line almost down to the wrist.

- Short—you may be a dreamer with a strong drive to achieve power and influence.
- Weak—could signal insecurity.
- Forked line—also called a travel line, it shows you have an adventurous spirit.
- Broken line—can mean you have gone through some major life changes.

THE FATE LINE

The fate line runs parallel to the life line and is near the middle of the hand. It shows how much energy you put toward achieving your goals.

- Straight—you are mature and know how to stand up for yourself.
- Faint—you may often feel anxious.
- Joined to the life line—you crave security.
- If the fate line starts half way up the palm, you may decide to change direction at some point in life.
- If it runs all the way up the palm, which is rare, it can mean you are inflexible.

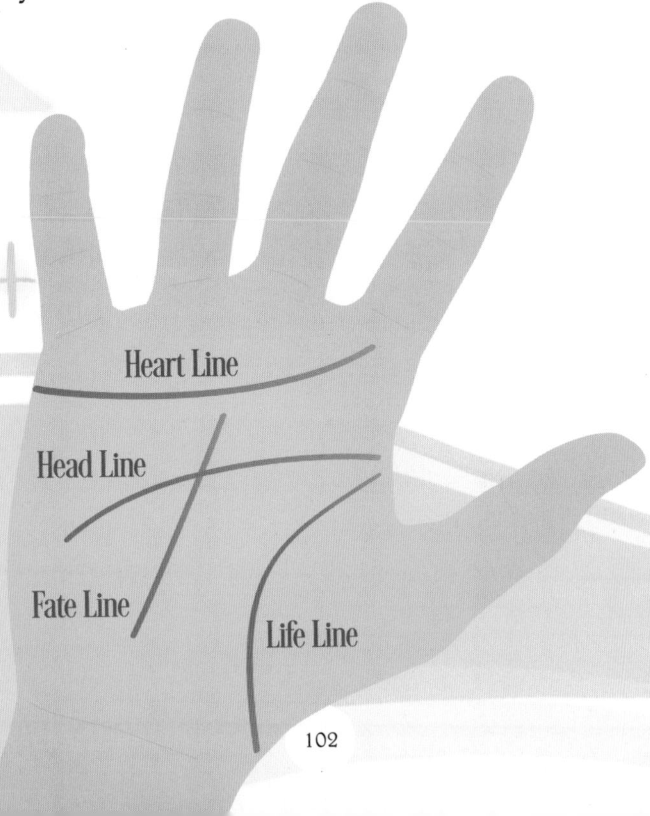

Heart Line

Head Line

Fate Line

Life Line

Runes

Introducing Runes

Runes—stones on which mystic symbols are engraved—can help you look deeply into your inner world, pinpointing fears and desires, and highlighting hidden factors that could shape the future.

The word "rune" means "secret writing." Casting runes began several thousand years ago in Scandinavia. The symbols represent birds, animals, and other things from nature. Today, the most popularly used set of runes is called the Elder Futhark set, also known as the Germanic Futhark. It is divided into three smaller sets (called aettirs) of eight runes each. Runes should be kept in a special bag when not in use.

The first set—or aettir—of runes is dedicated to Freyja, the goddess of love, war, and death. The second is dedicated to Heimdall, the guardian of the other gods and goddesses in the Norse tradition. The third is dedicated to Tyr, god of justice, law, war, and the sky.

CASTING THE RUNES

A simple way to cast runes for divination is with the three-rune spread.

- First, hold the question you want answered in your mind.
- Choose three runes from the bag and lay them out from left to right.
- The first rune indicates the situation, the second tells you the action required, and the third reveals the outcome.
- Look up the meaning of the stones using the following interpretations. Note the pronunciations of each.

Interpreting Runes

FREYJA'S AETTIR:

FEHU (PRONOUNCED: FEY-WHO)
Cattle–possessions and prosperity

Prosperity, wealth, and hard work. This energetic rune speaks to new opportunities and social success!

URUZ (PRONOUNCED: OO-ROOZ)
Ox–strength

Strength, courage, and overcoming obstacles. It speaks of good health, action, and deeper insights into your inner world.

THURISAZ (PRONOUNCED: THOO-RE-SAHZ)
Thorn–challenge or protection

Indicates change and avoiding conflict by following your instincts.

ANSUZ (PRONOUNCED: AHN-SOOZ)
A god–communication

Increased awareness of what the future holds; associated with inspiration, wisdom, aspiration, communication, spiritual progress, clear vision, and good health.

RAIDHO (PRONOUNCED: RYE-THO)
Riding–action

Indicates travel, either literal or a spiritual journey. Offers the chance for perspective and ease in unfortunate situations.

KENAZ (PRONOUNCED: KANE-AWZ)
Torch–inner wisdom

Represents the inner voice and inner strength. It indicates hope, and it helps dispel anxiety and fear.

GEBO (PRONOUNCED: GAY-BOH)
Gift–partnership

The rune stands for generosity. It also relates to contracts, love, and marriage. It promises balance and equality; it's an excellent rune to strengthen a relationship.

WUNJO (PRONOUNCED: WOON-YO)
Joy–pleasure

This rune brings comfort, joy, and the promise of harmony. It also warns of the dangers of extremes.

HEIMDALL'S AETTIR:

HAGALAZ (PRONOUNCED: HAW-GAH-LAWZ)
Chaos–change and destruction

Indicates uncontrolled forces wreaking havoc and disrupting plans, but also suggests that the crises will lead to inner harmony.

NAUTHIZ (PRONOUNCED: NOW-THESE)
Need–constraint

This rune says that conflict can be overcome by willpower. Embraces delays and restrictions; shows that fears must be faced.

ISA (PRONOUNCED: EE-SAH)
Ice–standstill or stillness

This rune underlines the messages of those around it. It speaks to frustration, blocked creativity, and a time to look inward. It can be worn to bring something to an end.

JERA (PRONOUNCED: YAIR-AH)
Year–harvest and life cycles

The rune of the harvest, when the results of your efforts can be gathered. It signals a happy, peaceful period. Wear it to encourage change.

EIHWAZ (PRONOUNCED: AY-WAHZ)
Yew–endings and mysteries

The yew tree represents the cycle of death and rebirth, so this rune means that natural endings are leading to new beginnings. It can bring change or help with difficulties.

PERTHRO (PRONOUNCED: PEAR-THROW)
Dice cup–initiation, the essence of one's being

The rune of what has yet to be revealed and of taking chances. Indicates mystery, secrecy, and psychic abilities; helps enhance divination.

ALGIZ (PRONOUNCED: AL-GEEZE)
Elk–sledge–protection

This rune signals help from unexpected places;
it encourages focusing energy toward the
greater good.

SOWILO (PRONOUNCED: SOH-WEE-LOH)
Sun–wholeness and potential

A rune of potential, success, energy, and
expansion. It promises that goals will be
achieved, and it increases strength and
encourages enthusiasm.

TYR'S AETTIR:

TIWAZ (PRONOUNCED: TEE-WAHZ)
Star–justice and victory

Signals esteem, justice, leadership, authority,
strength, and victory. It also suggests self-sacrifice.

BERKANA (PRONOUNCED: BEAR-KAH-NAH)
Birch–rebirth

The rune of birth, fertility, liberation, and mental,
physical, and personal growth. It promises new
beginnings and predicts success for ventures
underway; it can be used to help with a fresh start.

EHWAZ (PRONOUNCED: EH-WAHZ)
Horse–harmony

This rune predicts change for the better, harmony, teamwork, trust, and loyalty. It also confirms the meaning of the runes around it in a reading. Wearing it can bring you power.

MANNAZ (PRONOUNCED: MAN-WAHZ)
Man–the self, humanity, and tradition

This rune is concerned with intelligence, forethought, and creativity. When it appears, you can expect to receive help of some kind.

LAGUZ (PRONOUNCED: LAH-GOOZE)
Water–life forces and emotions

This rune signals the healing power of renewal. It emphasizes imagination and the mysteries of the unknown; stabilizes emotions; and helps uncover what is hidden. It also enhances psychic abilities and helps those who wear it to face their fears.

INGWAZ (PRONOUNCED: ING-OOZE)
The earth god–people

A rune of caring, love of family, and warmth. It predicts a period of rest and relaxation, when anxieties disappear. Wear it to encourage good health and to restore balance.

OTHALA (PRONOUNCED OWE-THA-LA)

Homestead–ancestral property

A rune of the home and whatever else is important in your life. It helps on spiritual and physical journeys, and it is a source of safety and of abundance. Wear it to help a project come to a conclusion and to strengthen family ties.

DAGAZ (PRONOUNCED: DAH-GAZ)

Day–integration

This rune suggests breakthroughs, awareness, and awakening. It promises clarity and says now is the time to embark on a new challenge! It helps bring about desired change and supports security, certainty, growth, and release.

WHAT ARE DREAMS?

The knowledge that can be acquired through dreams opens up a whole world of magic—if we have the ability to suspend disbelief and explore our creativity with courage!

Dreams can be seen as an expression of the unconscious creative self, which can contain messages that are either easy to understand—or come in symbols.

Exploring the creativity of dreams opens up different ways to approach your waking talents and abilities.

BETWEEN WAKING AND SLEEPING

The states between waking and sleeping (and sleeping and waking) are great for clearing your mind and focusing on your wishes and desires. During these periods, you can use incantations such as:

May the good I have done remain.
May the wrongs I have done be washed away.

This powerful statement can help clear your mind, so that your dreams can be magical and creative, rather than a "dumping ground" for the day's activities.

RELAXATION TECHNIQUE

Try this technique to become relaxed before sleep:

- Tense and release each area of your body for a few seconds, starting with your toes and moving all the way up to your head. Repeat three times.
- Next, tense your whole body at the same time and then let go completely. Repeat three times.

MEDITATION BEFORE SLEEP

A short meditation before bed can give you access to
your creative world of dreams; whereas, a short morning
meditation can help you understand dreams you may have
had the night before. To meditate, try this simple method.

- Choose a relaxing, quiet place where you won't be disturbed.
- Sit upright in a chair or on a cushion on the floor with your back supported.
- Soften your gaze or close your eyes, and begin to breathe evenly and deeply—inhale for a count of four, and exhale for a count of four.
- Once you've done this for a minute or so, extend your out-breath so it is a little longer than your in-breath.
- As you inhale, imagine you are breathing in peace; as you exhale, imagine you are releasing any stress from your body.
- Allow any thoughts that come up to just be— and then allow them to drift off. Don't cling to anything or fight it. Simply focus on your breath.
- Ask yourself to remember any dreams you may have had or contemplate a problem you wish to solve. You can also visualize something you would like to happen playing out in your mind.
- After 10 to 20 minutes, begin to move slowly and gently to come out of the meditation. Write down any thoughts or ideas that came up during your meditation.

DREAM JOURNALS

Keeping a dream journal can be a fascinating practice! Over time, you may notice that most or all of your dreams seem to be around a particular theme or that they follow a pattern. You can also record any ideas or visions that you have.

Dream Journaling Tips:

- Try to wake up naturally, without an alarm clock, so that you stay relaxed for as long as possible.
- Lie still for a moment and recall your dreams. Often, it is the most startling thing or feeling you will remember first, followed by more details.
- Note the date; then write the account of your dream (or make a voice recording).
- Give as much detail as possible, and write down anything that stands out as odd (animals, bizarre situations, etc.).
- Write or speak in the present tense: "I am standing on a hill," instead of "I was standing on a hill."
- Write down your feelings about the dream, as well as how you felt during the dream.

HOW TO HAVE A MAGICAL DREAM

This simple technique helps raise your consciousness and develops your ability to access your creative, magical mind. Make sure you do this regularly for the best results.

- Prepare for sleep by internally asking yourself to have a magical dream: "Tonight, my dream will be magical."
- Repeat this phrase out loud or in your head until you feel fully focused on it.
- Hold your intention to have a magical dream, and allow yourself to gently drift off to sleep.
- When you wake up, ask yourself if you were an observer or participant in your dream. How long did it seem to last?

In myth, Hypnos was the god of sleep. A sip from Hypnos' cup is said to send you into a blissful sleep until his mother, Nyx (Night), has fled the sky.

A SPELL FOR MAGICAL SLEEP

You will need a cup of chamomile tea; your dream
journal; a pen; and a crystal, such as jade, that
helps with dreams.

- Hold your cup of tea in both hands and say:

> Hypnos, Lord of Sleep, son of Night,
> Bless this cup and give me rest;
> That I may benefit from all your might
> And know forever what is best.

- Drink from the cup.
- Place the journal and pen close to your bed,
  with the crystal on top. Say:

> Morpheus, Morpheus, shaper of dreams,
> Crafter of light not all that it seems.
> Send me now images fit only for kings;
> Those that fulfill my deepest yearnings.
> Let me remember all that I learn;
> True to myself, to you I now turn.

- Relax into a deep, magical sleep and await
  developments!

Asking for the Dreams You Want

Once you've meditated regularly and have kept a dream journal for a while, you can start to ask for specific dreams to help you with an issue or to predict the future. Use the acronym "CARDS" to help jog your memory. This stands for Clarify, Ask, Repeat, Dream, and Study.

- Clarify the issue. Try to state the issue in positive language For example, "The best exam results are coming my way," instead of "I keep getting awful exam results."
- Ask the question using words like "who," "what," "why," "where," and "when" to help you formulate your · question. Example: "Who could help me improve my results?"
- Repeat your question multiple times to make sure it gets put into your subconscious mind.
- Dream and document. Use the relaxation and meditation techniques on pages 117–119 to help induce sleep. As you go to sleep, give yourself a dream command: "I will have a dream that will give me the answer to my question." Don't worry if your dream doesn't come right away—it might not come for several nights—so be patient.

- When you do have the dream, write down as much detail as possible.
- Study the dream. Examine the imagery, as well as details, clues, and hidden meanings. See if you can apply them to situations in your everyday life—and interpret the meaning of any symbols you see.

Once you've done this technique for a while, you'll be able to get even more creative. Soon you'll be able to ask questions such as, "What would happen if I did _____?"

This is the exciting process of making life more magical!

Index

ALWAYS REMEMBER THE ANSWERS COME NOT FROM THE ROCK, THE TEACUP, THE SHELL, OR THE CARDS. THE ANSWERS COME FROM YOU.

GWENDOLYN WOMACK

Other titles in the series:
Spells * Crystals * Astrology * Palm Reading *
Manifesting * Tarot * Spells and Charms